Stop Playing With a Sister's Heart

Shane'tta Rodmon

**Copyright @ 2019 Shanetta Rodmon
All Rights Reserved**

No part of this book may be reproduced or transmitted in any form or by any means, electronically or mechanically, including photocopying, recording, or by any information storage and retrieval system without permission from the author of this book.

All scriptural references are taken from the King James Version of the Bible or The Living Bible.

Credits

Photographer for the Cover
Mr. Shawn McPherson

Book Cover
Prophet Terrence Cruger

Editor
Spirit of Excellence Writing & Editing Services

www.TakeUpThySword.com

Table of Contents

Foreword

Dedication

Chapter 1   **God Created Man in His Image**

Chapter 2   **Let's Get Real**

Chapter 3   **Fatal Attraction**

Chapter 4   **Sister Got Game**

Chapter 5   **Man of God, Stop Tripping**

Chapter 6   **Just Keeping It Real**

Chapter 7   **The Heart**

Chapter 8   **Change is Coming**

Conclusion

About the Author

Foreword

It is my heartfelt desire that my brothers and sisters be set free from the things that have kept them in bondage. I am not trying to put my brothers down; I am only trying to help them to better understand us single sisters who desire to be respected and loved as Christ loves the church. This book is for the single men of God. Prayerfully, this book can help apostles, bishops, pastors, ministers, deacons as well as other men who profess to be Christians and are following the doctrine of Jesus Christ.

My brother, whatever your position is in the Body of Christ, I want to talk to you. Do not lay this book aside. Read it so you can gain full knowledge of the message God has given me to share with you. Allow this book to push you to a deeper place of understanding. Search within yourself to discover the king in you as you find your queen in this season. This book is not to put my brothers down but to help them better understand women's feelings, emotions and hearts. My goal is to educate my brother on how to care for a sister's heart. The Bible says in Proverbs 3:5-6, "Trust in the Lord with all thine heart; and lean not unto thine own understanding. In all thy ways acknowledge him, and he shall direct thy paths."

Dedication

This book is dedicated to all of my beautiful sisters who have ever been hurt or disappointed on this journey called love. I dedicate this to every woman who has ever shed a tear because their fragile heart had been torn in two at the hands of someone they loved and respected. This book is for all of my sisters who suffered at the hands of a man who she loved. I dedicate this book to women all over the world who have placed their trust in a brother and he hurt or manipulated the gift that God had given him.

My prayer is that every woman will be healed, delivered and set free as a direct result of coming in contact with this book. The Bible tells us in Psalm 34:18 that "The Lord is close to the brokenhearted and saves those who are crushed in spirit." My sisters and brothers, I believe that because of reading this book, your life will be forever changed and the broken heart you once had will be healed. After reading this book, you will recapture the joy and peace that once existed in your life.

God desires that all of His children be restored and replenished when they have a direct connection with the Word of God. Sit back and get ready to have a life-changing experience. If your heart has been played with, God is about to make you WHOLE again.

Genesis 1:26

Then God said, "Let's make mankind in our image, in our likeness, so that they may rule over the fish in the sea and the birds in the sky, over the livestock and all the wild animals, and over all the creatures that move along the ground"

Chapter 1

God Created Man in His Image

We are indeed made in the image of our Father. God created us in His image so we could have dominion over the earth and everything therein. This includes us having authority and dominion over our home and family as well. To walk in dominion means that He has given you and I power and authority regarding the union of marriage. God has ordained you to be the head of your families. As the husband, God has given you a responsibility to lead your family to Christ. God has given you a wife to be your helpmate and not a playmate.

God has entrusted the woman's heart to the man to care for her and to nourish her until death do you part. God created the woman as a tender flower to be adored in his beautiful garden of life. Brother, I am saying to you that as a man of God, you must have the heart to let her know your intention of courting her from the beginning. Before you open the door to her heart, you must already be prepared to love and cherish her all the days of your life. You must lay aside every weight that will drag her down as she submits to you. Do not just tell a woman what you think she would like to hear just to keep her hanging on until you decide what you are going to do with her. A woman is not an object but a beautiful creation created by God our Father.

When a woman is strung along and starts to feel like she is being played with, it will result in a spirit of rejection being planted into her heart. She may be dealing with that spirit from another relationship and this breeds a wild fire of problems to ensue in the relationship. I ask you, my brother, to count the cost before you take a sister's heart and mishandle it. I advise you to pray and seek God to know if this is the one whom God has chosen to be your wife. When you are in the process of finding a wife, it should not be treated like a shopping excursion - picking up what looks good and then when you get to the register, finding something else that looks better and abandoning it on the shelf to be put back as a return.

A mature man of God will know his wife when he sees her because he has already seen her in the spirit. The Bible says in Proverbs 18:22, "He who finds a wife finds a good thing and receives favor from the Lord."

I recommend that you watch her a while and pray for her to make sure this is the will of God. What the two of you bring to the table will help birth out the best in both of you.

Men, please do not just go on appearance alone when seeking a wife. She may have the bundles and the body but her boldness for Christ may be lacking. You must find a woman who has a heart after God. If there is not any love for God, keep seeking. If a woman does not have a heart for God, she will not have a heart for you. She may have other good qualities that attract your attention but will she be able to keep it? The only thing that will be able to sustain you, man of God, is a woman who wars in the spirit for you when you become weak in the spirit.

When we come to the full knowledge of God, we must not think as we did when we were in the world. Stop acting like you did B.C. = Before Christ.

When you were in the world, you may have caught any fish that was on your hook but once you decided to live for God, you have to live life according to His commandments. Men, do not get upset or distracted when a woman says that the Lord said you are their husband because there were times when men did the same thing, declaring wives when God had not spoken it to be so. Use wisdom in seeking and selecting a wife because marriage is a sacred covenant before God.

God presented Ruth to Boaz. Had Boaz not prayed and sought God for his wife, he would not have found her and he would have missed his blessing. Brothers, to be one hundred percent honest with you, there will be some women you will not have to waste your time on. You will know she is not the one right away. If you are courting a woman and you cannot see her in your long-term future, then don't do short-term things with her.

Don't play with someone's heart and expect not to reap what you have sown. Don't make promises to a woman if you don't have the intent of marrying her. Keep your proposals to yourself until you are firmly secure that she is the rib you are seeking as a life partner. Make sure she is the rib God has chosen for you.

My brother, you are created in God's image so the same loving heart that God possesses is the same heart you must carry. God created you with His lenses so you must see our sisters as the delicate flowers they are. God created a woman with inner strength and the ability to be a nurturer, but God gave a man strength that supersedes just inner strength – he has the power and ability to lead his family. A man was designed to be a woman's protector, provider and the caretaker of her heart and soul. The man is to take precious care of a woman's heart to keep her protected from all hurt, harm and danger.

My brother, honor and respect us all while you are seeking your wife. We all are potential wives for someone. If you damage us before we are found, it will make it harder on the next brother. The main thing we as women ask is that you do not string us along if you know we are not the one you desire to wed. After courting us and things do not go as God and you intended, please do not assassinate our character. Do not tell lies and make us seem like we are damaged and flawed when all we are seeking is validation and love. Continue to tell us the truth even if it may hurt us, and never keep us in the dark concerning your intentions for marriage.

If you are courting multiple persons let's know that before we assume that we are exclusively dating. Brother, if you have a heart after God, you will be straightforward and direct, withholding nothing that may hurt us in the process. Women are considered flowers in God's great garden. God loves His flowers and He is very careful about who He allows to handle them.

Man of God, we understand that God created you first. The Bible says in 1 Timothy 2:13, "For Adam was first formed, then Eve." God took a rib from Adam and made woman. This is why Adam said "bone of my bone and flesh of my flesh." Adam understood that this woman was made from his body. He had an understanding that Woman came from him and it was his responsibility to be very careful with her in every manner. This scripture alone confirms that God intended for man to take full responsibility for the woman who came solely from his innermost parts.

To take on this mandate, you, brother, must be strong in the Lord. It is time out for you playing the role of "Playboy." God is calling forth real men of God to care for His precious flowers in the garden. God is commanding you brothers to stand up and take your rightful place in the Kingdom of God, and prepare yourself for marriage. Men, it is no longer your choice to choose a wife but you must consult God in all your ways, and this includes finding your eternal soulmate.

The words says in Proverbs 3:5 Trust in the LORD with all thine heart; and lean not unto thine own understanding. Brothers, you must not chose a woman because she has a good job, formal education, her own home, money in the bank, prestige in the community, a title in the church or a fashion model's body. You must look at the inward parts of a woman and let God confirm that she is the one. In the Old Testament, it was reported that when a man considered marrying a woman, he brought a dowry to the woman's family. The times in which we are living now, all you hear from men is what she is able to bring to the table. I am not saying that you should not look for a woman to have her own independence and finances, but never look for a woman to take care of you.

Your wife is considered a good thing and she will come into the marriage with some good things. The blessing for you, as the scripture says, is that you will obtain favor from the Lord because of having her. So with that being said, your reward will come from God and not her. When you obtain your favor, she will come with the ability to lift you up and be in tune with your spirit man. She will build you up and not tear you down. Marriage is a ministry. It is two people joining their gifts, talents and love for God to help to exalt the Kingdom of God.

There was a slogan many years ago that said WWJD = What Would Jesus Do? Well my dear brother, I believe that Jesus would seek the heart of a woman to see if He was in her heart. I believe that Jesus would go to His Father and seek counsel and guidance. I believe that Jesus would be open and honest with others and not try to manipulate and mislead them. I know that the God I serve would not lead others on when He knew He had no desire to wed.

Keep in mind, my brother, that the way you interact with a woman has a huge impact on her future relationships if you decide not to wed her. Be careful not to plant a seed of hurt and pain in God's garden. If you have found yourself in your past not operating out of a spirit of love, compassion, honesty and respect for a woman, you need to repent and ask God for forgiveness so you can be given another chance to find healthy love and your rib-mate.

After repenting, tell the person you hurt or misguided that you are sorry. If left untreated, the wounds can really delay growth in a sister. When you have left her wounded, it is hard for another brother to help her heal without her wounds being open and exposed again. Consider the plea for repentance and help a sister heal. For when we all heal, the Kingdom can rejoice.

One day I was watching TBN, and this new worship leader disclosed that he had made a list of what kind of wife he wanted in his life. He was afraid of getting married. God told him one day to let Him see the list. God told him he could do it his way or he could allow Him to bless him with a wife. God desires that we allow Him to be a part of our every decision. The Word tells us in

Proverbs 3:6 that in all your ways, acknowledge God and He will direct your path. This includes marriage too.

I recall a man of God telling me that he was engaged to marry a woman. He had a ring custom designed for her. He paid a large amount for it. He was sure she was the one. God spoke to him and said, "You didn't pray and ask me if this was your wife." God told him that he had chosen to do his own thing without His consent. After repenting to the Lord, he called the engagement off. I know God will leave you to yourself if you choose to still do your own thing against His will. God will not bless your mess.

My brother, before you approach a woman for marriage or to be engaged, you must be sure that God has given you consent. Remember that God said that everything He made was good, and this includes your ordained wife. When God created man, He looked down on it and knew that it was good for man and woman to be together in holy matrimony. When God created man for woman, He placed character, strength, passion, love, gentleness and kindness that were needed for the institution of marriage.

God chose Eve for Adam because He knew she would be good for him. When God took Adam and put him in a deep sleep to extract his rib, the purpose was to create Eve. The rib is symbolic in the union between Adam and Eve. In Genesis 2:23, it says: "And Adam said, This is now bone of my bones, and flesh of my flesh: she shall be called Woman, because she was taken out of Man." God said that man would receive favor when he committed to a wife. Adam was not worried about Eve's bank account, where she lived or any of her materialistic characteristics. God intended for the unity between husband and wife to be solid and based on building the Kingdom together.

My brother, when seeking a wife, make sure you are ready to lead a woman. Jesus was a man who always lived by example. He lived and walked the earth with the assignment of pleasing His Father. Jesus always prayed and said that man should always pray as well. Being made in His image, you should show some of the characteristics of Christ.

God's character is so important. His character must be displayed out of the heart of man. God was a man and He never disrespected a woman. In every encounter He had with a woman, He treated her with respect and love. As a godly man, your character should be different from the men of the world. Your potential wife should see the God in you and be willing to follow you as you follow Christ.

When pursuing Christ, do not act on your emotions. The Word tells us in Psalm 46:10 to be still and know that He is God. Sometimes we make decisions based on our emotions and this is not a God-move but a flesh-move. When seeking a wife, you must go to the most holy places in God. The throne room is where you will receive your answers. Man of God, your obedience to God will help you to find the right bride. God will give you a conformation in your spirit. But I know that no marriage, engagement or proposal for marriage will be without issues or problems because the devil hates unity.

The book of Proverbs talks about obtaining wisdom and how valuable it is. Wisdom is the principal key to sustaining anything that God has created. The Holy Spirit is wisdom. If you have the Holy Spirit, you have wisdom that will help to sustain your marriage. As you grow in God, your wisdom will increase. God has given you many promises as it relates to marriage. Follow the instructions He has given you.

My brother, before you make a lifetime commitment to God and His daughter, make sure you have been delivered from your flesh and issues so you do not taint the union God is about to bless you with. You can be made completely whole as you take on the mantle of marriage. Let God heal you from the inside out. Do not be a stowaway, be a true part of God's family. Let God love you and show you the inner most parts of your heart and soul so you don't carry all your baggage into your covenant relationship.

Let God teach you how to be a husband and how to treat your wife. The Word says in Proverbs 14:12, "There is a way which seemeth right unto a man, but the end thereof are the ways of death." Let God produce life in you today. For you are not worldly men but men of God. Bring forth good fruits in the Body of Christ. Understand that sleeping around in the church is wrong as well. Doing whatever you want is not permitted in the Kingdom of God. There is a cost for disobedience. Everything you do will be accounted for when you stand before God.

John 8:32

And ye shall know the truth, and the truth shall make you free.

Chapter 2

Let's Get Real

In this chapter, I will be dealing with single pastors. I want to talk to you as it relates to my personal experiences with this particular subject matter. I feel that I can help the men of God that have the position of pastor, minister, apostle, evangelist or bishop to better know how to care for us sisters. I want to start by saying this: You, man of God, are an awesome, mighty man of God, very powerful and strong. We look up to you all and respect you as not just as a spiritual leader but also as a Kingdom builder.

I want to talk to you about Ruth and Boaz. I have heard pastors say that the women in their church are their daughters. For this reason, they cannot and will not marry anyone in their church. What I was told is that this would cause problems and people would leave the church. Well, let me take a stroll down the life of Ruth and Boaz and tell you what God showed me.

When Ruth went into Boaz' field to work, there was already young and old women working in his field and they knew he was single and wanted him for themselves. One of the key factors is that Boaz' field represented the church and the people who worked in his field represented his members, for he was the master and overseer over them. When Ruth showed up, she became a member also. There was something about Ruth that stood out that the man of God was attracted to. Boaz didn't let the fact that there were other women working in his field and had their eyes on him. He knew there were some hoping, praying and backstabbing each other.

He knew what was going on. He knew they were gossiping about Ruth and saying negative things, they even tried to use manipulation. God placed an anointing on Ruth that attracted Boaz. He knew when he first saw her that she was the one, but I believe that he was afraid to even make a move towards her. He knew that there were others who had their eyes on him for a long time who had worked his fields for years.

I am sure that there were some he had around him and when they saw he was showing interest in Ruth, they began to come to him saying, "You know Ruth is not one of us and I don't think it would be wise to take her as your wife. She doesn't have a good background." Because of where she came from, they made these assumptions about her.

Let me say this to you, man of God: even if you go outside of the church and get someone, some of your female members may still leave your church because they were there for the wrong reasons. It is your responsibility to teach them and not play with their heart by making them think that you are interested in them when you are not. You just don't want them to leave your church. You want to gain control over them. Man of God, teach the women from the pulpit that when God shows you who your wife is, whether she is in that church or not, you will obey God and not man.

There is a price to pay when you obey people and not God. Look back at King Saul when he disobeyed God. Remember what great price he paid. Even you as a pastor need to also protect God's daughters' hearts as well. Do not play with their hearts. Protect them from the wolves out there, and don't make them think you want them when you don't. Help lead them to Christ and He will lead them to the man of God whom He has anointed and appointed for them.

Just teach, correct, lead and guide the women in your church. We need someone to stand up for us and say to the men of God that they need to seek God before they make their move; and if they pray to God, He will answer. Man of God, don't jump from woman to woman just because you can. This is not the character of God at all, for you were created in His image. Please be very honest with the women in your church. Don't lead them on as if you have any intention of marrying them.

Some sisters are honest, faithful and true. As women, we are praying for godly husbands; we don't want just anything or anybody. We have given up our worldly ways and have ceased from doing things our own way in order to attract a godly husband. We have surrendered ourselves to God—not just to show the man we are his wife, but for God to show us our husbands through prayer and fasting. If we do not pray and fast, then anyone could just walk up and say, "God showed me that you are my wife." We are living in a time when the women of God must hear and know as well. This is why so many women have been wounded and hurt. We have just left it all up to the men to just show up and say, "You're the one."

Remember that God said in the last days, He would pour out His spirit upon all flesh. There are many wolves out there as well as in the church. I have heard people on the outside say, "I should go to church and get a woman because that is where all the good ones are." But they come to church and defile God's daughters and cause them to follow a lie rather than hear the truth. The truth is that he is not the one and not being truthful. Stop now!

When you look in the Bible and study it, you will see that God has a standard. God does not view us as ministry material. God is God and has all power to change people. Let's look at Queen Esther. When you look in the Bible, she was not queen material. She was a poor Jewish girl whose parents had died. Her uncle raised her. God knew her before the foundation of the world, and He knew who Esther would be.

Men of God, stop being controlled by money and people. Start being controlled by the Holy Spirit. God still ordains marriages, so look to Him and not to yourself. There is someone out there teaching that a woman should have money and this and that. Let me go back to the Bible as I study and understand the Word of God: It shows that every time a man of God got ready to go get his wife, he paid a dowry to the woman's family. I know that we are living in different times but the Word of

God says that He is the same yesterday, today and forever, and He cannot change.

Stop looking at her finances but look to God because He said that the most important thing is that you are to seek Him for yourself and find out if this is the one and not if she has a bank account. There are good praying women out there who don't have large bank accounts or any account at all but they love God. It is sad that the Body of Christ has to act like the world in picking a wife. Women of God have to have a profile now. It is no longer if she loves God or has a relationship with Him.

Let's get back to God's standards when looking for a wife. If you go by what she has and not by what God said, then you will eventually pay the price. Let's look at how God blessed some mighty men in the Bible and how they married women who didn't have anything: Sarah became a mother of all nations. Esther became queen and saved her people. Ruth gave birth to Obed who was Jessie's father who was King David's father. Rachel gave birth to Joseph who became ruler/governor of Egypt. Hannah gave birth to the prophet Samuel. Mary gave birth to our Lord and Savior Jesus Christ. Elizabeth gave birth to John the Baptist. All of these women started out with nothing but God had a plan for their life. If Joseph had not listened to the angel of the Lord, then Jesus would not have been born to them and their names would not appear in the Bible today.

Men of God, let's get it together and do things God's way like the mighty men of old and not the world's way like the rich and famous. There is destiny and purpose in all God's women. When He created them from the man's rib, He created them with purpose on the inside of them. He created the woman to be man's helpmate. He created them to help push you into your destiny, strengthen you, call you lord and encourage you. The woman was created to pray you through and many more things. A praying wife does what money can't do all the times, and that is why you man of God need a praying wife to cover you in prayer and stay on their face before the Lord on your behalf. I talked about this in Chapter 1 and I am back on this subject again in this chapter.

God wants you to get an understanding of His Word not just to read it and do what you please with it. In Genesis 2:22, it says that after creating Eve from Adam's rib, God brought her to him. This tells me even more that God does play a very important part in you finding your wife. Just because God said "he who finds a wife" in Proverbs 18:22 doesn't mean that He has left that choice totally up to you. God said in Jeremiah 1:5 that He knew you before He created you in your mother's womb. This means that your life has already been set. If you go along the path God has set, you will get the right wife. If you do it your way, then you will get the wife your flesh wanted.

God brought Eve to Adam so all God is saying is that when He brings your wife, you must have eyes to see her in the spirit and ears to hear God confirm it to you. Learn to hear from God yourself by developing a relationship with Him. Now let's go deeper: God is no respecter of persons so why do you, my brother? You tell yourself that the woman you have chosen is of God and you know it is not, picking and choosing by what a woman has or doesn't have.

God said that when you find your wife (when God shows her to you), you will obtain favor from Him. What does favor mean? That means God is going to bless you. After God brought Eve to Adam, he was able to see and know that she was whom God had ordained to be his wife. The woman of God must come out of your rib. Allow God to put you into a deep sleep and let Him bring forth that woman of God out of you that He created for you.

God knew what kind of woman Adam needed. He put everything Adam needed into Eve. Even though she made some mistakes, she managed to get it right. Eve even knew how to minister to her husband through personal care, household duties and through prayer. For this, women must be able to keep you lifted up in prayer when times are good or bad. She must be able to encourage you. She must help bring forth your ministry in prayer.

Just being attractive or having a lot of money is not good enough. A woman can look good but make sure her insides are even prettier. Do not worry about if she has money. Obey God's Word and let Him bless you and your wife. This is why prayer is so important in finding your helpmate.

Prayer allows God to be a part of the process and lead you in the right direction in order to find the right wife. God in no way meant for man to leave Him out of this very important part of his life. God wants you to have the best.

There is one of God's best for each of God's men. Let God create her from your rib and then you too can say that she is bone of your bones and flesh of your flesh. When God sees you heading down the wrong path to the wrong woman, He will try to stop you. It is something we want and it is just our flesh and not God. In order to protect us, He must stop us from making a mistake. If we refuse His help, then He will let us have it. This will overcome you and God will remind you that He tried to stop you. He showed you all the signs but you did it your way.

My brothers, if you ask for someone's hand in marriage but didn't pray or seek God and realize you are making an mistake, please do not be afraid to call it off. A friend of mine said he asked this woman to marry him and had not prayed or sought the Lord about it first. Then the Lord told him that she was not the one. Before asking someone for her hand in marriage, you need to ask for God's guidance. My friend called the engagement off in obedience to God. It is better to obey God than get out of God's will and pay the price.

Pastor, it is important that you have the right woman of God standing by your side. God knows that He has placed a great woman of God to stand by you; He has placed someone in your life to protect the mantle He has over your life. Just as God has placed you to be a covering over His people, He is also the covering over you. Man of

God, He safety guards you the same way you are called to secure His people.

God will not pick a wife for you who will not be a good helpmate. Stop listening to the "big time" pastors (I don't mean any disrespect to them for they are who God says they are). Stop listening to them saying she should have this and that. The truth is they did not check out the one's they are married to. They said that God showed them that this was the one. This is why their marriage is successful. All this stuff about money and fame—watch out because you may not get what you thought.

Allow God to bless you as He did Adam. Yes, I have made one mistake but God already knew that it would happen. Remember God created Eve from Adam's rib. We know that it was good for God said that every and good and perfect gift comes from above. Man of God, you will receive the perfect gift when you allow God to choose her for you. All you have to do is watch and pray; the Lord God will do the rest. Remember that God is able to turn that woman's credit around and cause her to blow up with great wealth. You will miss it because you are looking at where she is right now in the natural. Man of God look in the spirit, seek God's answer and not man's advice.

God said in Isaiah 55:8-9 that your thoughts neither are your ways, my ways saith the Lord. Far as the Heavens are higher than the earth, so are my ways, and my thoughts than yours. Stop trying to think or outthink God. Just submit your ways and thoughts unto Him for He knows just what and whom you need. You talk a good game about how awesome God is when preaching it from the pulpit; but when it comes to your mate, you size her up and pick someone with money and not that sister who is in love with God—that praying sister.

Whatever you seek after, you just might get it. Let me stop right here and say this: just because she is a praying woman doesn't mean she is still not a woman who doesn't know what to do in the bedroom. Some men of God are somewhat afraid of women who pray all the time and it seems they don't do anything or go anywhere. We do have a life... Well, we do have a life hidden in Christ Jesus that is pleasing unto Him until He sends us our mate. After we are found, we then become that man of God's wife and our preparation for marriage has been fulfilled.

Man of God, you have free will during this selection process. God will bring her and present her to you. It is up to you to hear the Word of God and obey. Stop looking in the natural and start seeing in the spirit. Where God is going to take you and do through your obedience is going to blow your mind. He is going to reward you for marrying the one He handpicked, purposed and created just for you. The woman God chose for you has everything in her to meet your needs and more. He put everything inside of her to perfectly fit your needs and ministry.

Many years ago, marriages were arranged. When a princess was promised a prince at birth and they didn't have a choice, they simply had to obey the orders of their parents and trust it was going to be a good match. It could have been for business or to gain more power. Whatever the reason, that woman was trained from birth and taught to serve her prince (or shall I say, her king in our case). She was taught what he liked and didn't like. At the appointed time, she was brought before the king, and then the engagement began.

Man of God, you need a woman whom God has prepared for you who has been through years of preparation. God is now ready to bring her before the king who has been chosen for her to reign with in the earth to bring God's glory into the earth. She is now ready to go forth with you in power and strength to win many to the Lord while serving you as her pastor and lord.

Pastor, you are put in a powerful position to lead, guide, teach, encourage and so much more. Do not abuse or misuse the daughter God has given you to care for. I know you want someone to share your life with, but you must make sure she is from God and not the choosing of your flesh before you move in towards her heart. It is your job to protect the daughters God has given you. Man of God, you can pick from among your own garden; there is nothing wrong with this. For in time past, men were told to go to their own people to choose a wife. You just have to make sure through prayer that she is the one.

While living in Chicago, I met a woman of God who was a member of a church and the pastor was single. He began to pursue this woman. He would have her go with him to church services by his side. He was leading her on but his inner circle started to get jealous, began to pray against her and turn him against her. It became so intense that it started to make her feel crazy. This small group of people who called themselves intercessors and assistant pastors were only Jezebels trying to control the man of God and the will of God. This almost destroyed a very precious woman of God. She had to leave the church and through this, she was able to regroup and gain her strength again.

Pastors, do not start what you are not willing to finish; do not start your pursuit and then back up. This can cause great problems in your church. It is not whether you are married outside or inside the church, it's about hearing from God and getting a sure word from Him before you start something that you decide later you are willing to finish or complete. God has our entire life planned out.

The Word of God says that He orders our steps, which means our life. We just need to follow His plan and not our own. This is why it is so important that we have a very intimate relationship with Him and know His voice. The Word says that the Lord's sheep know His voice and another they will not follow. Stop making excuses for your actions and follow the plan of God for your life.

The package God shows you may not look, walk, sound, act or have what you think they should have. Man of God, in no way am I calling you a failure. What I am saying is that some of you along the way have missed God in finding a wife. This is one of the reasons that marriages in the Body of Christ are failing. Some of you have done things according to the world's standards. I say to you, go back to God's Word with much prayer and fasting. To understand what your Father in Heaven is really saying to you about a wife and how He is a part of the process, seek His Word about marriage.

Go back to Adam and Eve and look at the process and care God took to form Adam's wife Eve. Look at the process in which He formed her from Adam's rib. The key point is that God did it and Adam trusted God to create just what he knew Adam needed.

Even with all her little hang-ups, God created her. It should not be about stuff and things in choosing a wife, it should be about God and Him knowing what is best for you.

Stop checking out statistics and possessions of others. Look to HIM who is the Author and Finisher of our faith. Our faith in Him is to trust His plans for our life. The Lord will guide you and never leave you. He brought you this far even though it may have been hard. The hills you may have climbed and the valleys you may have went down were only to see you rise above it all safely in His arms. It is important for you to tell the sisters in your church the truth and not be afraid of them leaving your congregation. For God said He adds to the church daily as He sees fit.

Back in 2002, I thought I heard the Lord tell me that this man of God was the one. I talked to some women of God who said, "Yes, it's God," and that

God said for me to move to Chicago. I moved without seeking the Lord about it. I even had the women to pray for me for reassurance.

Well the sisters at this man's church were not having it. They would gather themselves together and begin to attack me through prayer. I do not know if they thought they were praying God's will or not. However, it was an all-out attack on me. My body came under attack through those prayers. It was so bad that when it was prayer night service, I would become so sick that I could not get off my couch to go. On those nights, it was close contact in small groups so if he looked or talked to me, they would start praying. I knew I was in a battle and it was not prayer service but war service just to stay alive.

One woman warned me because the same women had attacked her when this man pursued her. She said that not only had the women come after her, but also the assistant pastor. He was in fear of losing his position, When God had planned to give him his own ministry. He also didn't want the pastor to get married. He was the one who would tell the pastor who his wife was. He had an influencing spirit that was over the man of God.

I became so sick that I could not even be in a room with the lights on. The pressure was great. When I heard the Lord say to me leave, I obeyed and the sickness I was experiencing went away. I know that some of you are saying, "This is why it is not good to marry outside of your church." I say to you that God can and will place your wife right under you. Yes, they brought her in to the place as Ruth was brought unto Boaz's country.

However, they all were set- ups to bring about the will and plan of God in the earth. This is one of the ways that God works: He creates our situations so that He can move on our behalf. His intention is to get our attention so we will praise Him and bring glory to Him. The Lord told me that any prayer that is not prayed according to His will is witchcraft.

Man of God, set the women straight in your church; tell them the truth. Do not keep them hanging on until you make up your mind or so they wont leave your church you will have to give account for how you handle what God gave you.

I was talking to this man of God and he said something so key to me. It stood out because it confirmed what God had also told me. God told me why so many women run after one man and why they all think God told them this is their husband.

God is not just going to tell the man, he will tell the woman too. If this one-sided concept were true, then we would marry anyone who walked up to us and said, "The Lord told me that you are my spouse." God talks to women too, not just men. I know that He confirm His Word through the man. Some women are emotional and if a man pays the slightest bit of attention to us, we run off and start saying that he wants us and he is the one when it is really just our emotions or flesh. So as I said, I ran off to another state; it was about 1,200 miles away. I was thinking that God said he was the one. I would talk to another man of God and he would ask, "Are you sure God said he is the one?" I would tell him I was sure because of this and that but in my heart, I knew it was not so. My heart knew better because before leaving for that city, God tried to stop me. He was trying to get my attention and stop me from going. It is so very important that we obey the voice of God.

Man of God, you may have five to ten women come to you but it is up to you to seek the matter out. I know there are instances where some men already know the first time they meet a woman that she is their wife. Even in this situation, you still need to follow it up with prayer. Marrying the right woman is very important to your ministry. You can be unequally yoked right in the Body of Christ with a believer.

What I mean by this is that God has you set on one path and you're with this person who says they are with you until you are married and you then find out that God's will for your life is different from hers. She has her own plans and is not willing to support you, or pray you through or support the ministry. She could care less if the birthing of God's destiny in you comes out or not.

One of the key things I say to you is to check out if she has a prayer life and a heart for God. Is she intimate with God? Does she know the voice of God? In addition, it's not about how much money she has and or what type of job she has. For if God is in the plan and you are humble, He will give you what you need when you leave it up to Him, and like Mary said , "Lord be it unto me as you have spoken."

I know I am a woman writing this book but God gave it to me to do as I see it from a women's point of view. I myself have gone through and watched God bring me out right where He wanted me to be. I know He is not done with me but He has placed a word in me for this time to share with the men of God. Please do not look at the fact that I am a woman; just hear the instructions as God has allowed me to write them to you. He wants you to apply them when dealing with His daughters. I do not know everything but I can give you from my experiences and what God revealed to me as He began to reveal this book. This book is to help others walk with God through this process and not face it alone.

My prayer is that you will walk with Him every day so that when He is speaking, you will not miss His voice and do your own thing. I pray you act on what He is telling you to do. Your obedience to God is everything. The Bible tells us that we should follow God as dear children. The blessing doesn't come because you are such a wonderful speaker, or you know your Word better than everybody else. It comes because of your obedience to God. Because of Adams disobedience to God, he still had to be held accountable for the actions of his wife. For God made the man the head over the woman, and God gave him specific instructions.

Through prayer, seek God; no surface prayers are allowed. You must pray from your inner belly where the inner man lives. Pray until you get a breakthrough from God. God knows when you really want to get an answer from Him or are desiring to do it your own way. God has the answer to each one of our prayers. Just invite Him in to know His will and plan for your life. Remember He said, "Behold I stand at the door and knock." He needs you to let Him in. God is light and His light shines on all things. God knows all things; He just reveals it to us if He wants to.

So, my brother, why won't you trust Him? Let Him give you what you need and who you need to stand by your side. God has to condition your heart to function right; won't you let him do it? Pastors, you are a blessing from God; do not abuse your position. Respect the women of God. Do not take a Mack Truck and run over her heart.

God has the right woman for you if you would be patient and wait for Him.

In addition, stop going by the world systems, for we are in the world but not of this world. Therefore, we must do things according to His Holy Word. Look at the Bible; God did things differently even when putting marriage together. Who knows the mind of God? I say, those who seek Him and obey Him. You all are awesome men of God, and He has placed great calls on your life. Stay positioned in God. Let go and let Him manifest things in the natural for you. He did not need us to create the heavens and the earth; He did it without us. The world turned out beautiful. God knows what each one of us needs.

I had a wonderful, awesome man of God who I fell head over heels for overnight. I was deeply in love with him; I was crazy about him. I asked him twice to tell me that he was not interested in me but both times, he refused to say it to me. He did not know what God was going to tell him about me. He did not know that I needed him to release me because I was just so messed up in love with him. I just needed him to release me so that I could move on with my life. I understood what he was saying but he didn't know the main reason why I was asking. I would stop asking him this question for about four to six months and I would pick up from where I left off. Let me clarify something: I know some Kingdom men think, "Oh, how did she fall in love that easily?"

Let's stroll back through the Bible and look at some men who fell head over heels for women. Jacob in Genesis 29:1-11 shares how when he first saw Rachel, he moved the stone away for her to water the sheep, and then he kissed her and wept. When you take a walk through this story, you will see that he served his father-in-law for 14 years in order to have her as his wife. This tells me that he was head over heels in love with this woman and was willing to work as long as it took to have her. Just rolling away that stone said he was in love at first sight.

Jacob's father Isaac didn't get to pick his wife (see Genesis 24:1-67). His father Abraham sent his eldest servant to choose a wife for him. The Bible said that Isaac went and meditated in the evening time and lifted up his eyes and saw the camels coming. Rebekah lifted up her eyes and when she saw Isaac, she was lifted off the camel. To sum it up, they fell in love from their first encounter.

There is nothing wrong with falling in love at first sight or falling in love with someone who told you how they felt about you. When God sets something in motion, then He already approves it. It is time to stop trying to figure out how and when to do it. Sometimes you can put things off too long when God has already approved you to move forward. Man of God, stop dragging your feet. Pick up your feet and move forward into your destiny.

A man of God that I knew in Chicago. I stated earlier in this chapter that I went out there thinking he was the one. I had these women around me telling me he was the one and to go for it girl. When they just wanted me to get out of town. I will not say what their motives were right now. I will be dealing with that in my next book. While I was up there, I would often call him back and talk to a Man of God who is a pastor as well.

I needed to get some feedback from someone else to see what he thought about the situation and what I should do. He stated to me that if it were him he would not marry anyone from his congregation. He said it would cause conflict in the church and the people would leave.

The pastor in Chicago was married in 2007 and married outside of the church. The women at his church before he got married was sending me nasty emails.

After he got married, the women left the church saying God told them to leave. It was all because they wanted him for themselves. When they saw that this was not going to happen they left.

Many of them were only there for him not because God had placed them there. Stop worrying about the women in your church and how they are going to feel and react.

Soon as they leave your church, they will find another Man of God to prey on and try to hinder the will of God in his life.

Don't mislead the women in your church but tell them the truth.

If God has shown you your wife within the church, feel free to date them without feeling guilty.

God will bring the right people and weed out the wrong ones. When you obey his commandments.

Do not get discouraged when people leave your church call it spring-cleaning, God is only trying to bring your ministry to full maturity.

The intent of God is to manifest what has been hidden to those outside the church walls.

What I am about to say is not to all of you, just to the ones who know you still have problems. Please don't misunderstand me: Some of you men of God still have the player in you and you are not willing to grow up. You love the attention you get from the women in your church or should I say any females. You love playing mind games; this is a part of mind control. When the title of this chapter says Let's Get Real, that is what it means.

Let's draw out your dirt and little secrets that your other pastor friends do not know about. Let's draw them out to bring deliverance unto you. You can't make up your mind nor can you bring closure to your appetite for women. Stop suppressing it and allow God to deliver you from it. Everybody doesn't have to know, but you must do something about it before it destroys you and your ministry.

You are having a hard time making up your mind not knowing who, what and when. In this struggle, you're having with yourself, you are having a hard time. Be honest with yourself and them. Stop playing with a sister's heart. If God has told you a specific woman is your wife, then let her know. If you really care about yourself, your ministry and the woman whom God has placed before you, you will want the best for everyone involved.

However, this is not always the case in the church. The selfish spirit most times takes over and no one wins but the devil. When we deny ourselves, then the true will of God will come through. Man of God, stay connected to God. He will always order your steps. Be patient and wait for God to move.

Get rid of that Play Boy spirit; this is very important. This serves as a warning: if you do get married and have not dealt with your whoremonger spirit, you will destroy your marriage and ministry. Pay attention to women who are attention-seekers and will do anything to draw your attention or take your kindness and caring spirit as "he wants to be in a relationship with me."

I am talking from my own experiences. I was in a place where I thought a man was interested in me. I did not want him to hug me at all. This was because I knew how I felt about him. My emotions would run away with me. In order to keep a level head, I could not allow him to embrace me. I do not really know how it happened, but I fell hard for him. Was it his kindness toward me? Was it his gentleness or the way he treated me that made me become attracted to him?

I do know that hugging him for me had taken my emotions to another level. I allowed myself to go to that level. To him, it was just a hug and nothing more. Hugging can be a part of intimacy; it can speak volumes. To me, it said, "I am ready to go to the next level of commitment." If you are not sure, then do not move in close; for if she cares about you, she will then open her heart up to you. This is a tragedy waiting to happen. Watch what you say and if you say it then explain what you are saying. Do not allow her to think something is true if it is not your intentions.

My brother, let's count up the cost and remember that whatsoever you sow, you also reap. God is no respecter of persons; from the pulpit to the back door, it goes for all the men of God so you are not exempt.

Proverbs 18:22

He that findeth a Wife, findeth a good thing, and obtaineth favor of the Lord

Chapter 3

Fatal Attraction

This chapter is called fatal attraction because I want to talk to my single men of God about the choices that you make without seeking God first concerning who your wife is. Some of you brothers know what I am talking about; it equates to the sting of a black widow's bite. What I mean by that is you have been married before, more than one or two times. I know that God said "he who finds a wife" but let's just look at that for a minute. When God said for you to find a wife don't think He did not want to also play a part in you finding this wife.

Okay let's look at it like this: There was a man named Job who had a wife and when things began to go bad in their life, instead of standing by him, she criticized him and told him to curse God and die. Job didn't have to get rid of her; God did it for him. We can also look at David. David's wife told him that he looked stupid dancing out of his clothes before the people. Oh, yes, also look at King Ahasuerus in his marriage to Vashti. I know he was not a godly man but wait, I am going somewhere with this...

Now let's go back to Job: I don't know what drew him to her because the Bible does not tell us this. I want to deal with her character, faithfulness and loyalty; he certainly could not count on her when things were going bad.

Look at David's wife. She was not a woman who stood by her man in his decisions. If she was a woman who reverenced God, she would have understood why David was praising God like he was. She was not an encourager or a supporter. If

David's wife had to tell the story, she would say that he should have been ashamed of himself and to her, he was making a fool of himself.

King Ahasuerus' wife was a woman who showed no respect for her husband. She was a woman who did her own thing. She had a rebellious spirit. She would never be like Sarah who called her husband "lord."

I would like to stop right here for a minute and say that in no way does finding a wife give you the right to hurt your sisters in the Lord. I am not putting everything on you men of God; I am just talking to the ones who like to play games and let them know that our God is not pleased. If you have done this or you are doing it, then you need to get it right. God is very concerned with what happens to His daughters. He said that the woman is the weaker vessel and that you are to protect her from the wolves in sheep's clothing.

Let me share about the fatal attraction spirit. Even when Esau who take a wife from another tribe he did, this and it caused him to lose his birthrights. In the Word of God, it says there was grief upon Isaac and Rebekah (Genesis 26:35). God does give you the right to choose a wife but not without Him leading and guiding you to her. When you do not put God in it or even pray about it, this can be dangerous. Having the wrong woman beside you can be very damaging and dangerous to you, man of God.

When you choose a woman outside of the will of God, she could eventually make you cry and even wish you had never met or hooked up with her in marriage. She will make you pray all night long. You will even start saying to God, "this woman you gave me…" Then God will respond back with, "No, that is the woman you picked." Walking outside the will of God can cause damage to your health, your mind, your ministry and your character. Man of God, you could get to a place where you think you are losing your mind because the pressure is so great on you.

Stop profiling the women and checking out their bank accounts because you just might get what you are looking for. Yes, that's right. What you are looking for. When you are checking her out, check for her godly character and godly creditability. This type of attraction can cause you to be ashamed in the streets, church, community and family gatherings. Observe the woman you are "picking" closely. Sometimes when you listen to others, they may be able to tell you what kind of person your wife really is. People will discuss with you the good and the bad concerning a person but the true judgment should always come from God.

Finding a wife is not a game. When seeking a wife, do not seek after her flesh. Flesh gets old but the

Word of God and living holy is eternal. Man of God, only through prayer and supplication should you make your requests unto to God and get the final answer concerning your godly wife. Brother, get on your face before God, turn down your plate and seek God. You may have to stay up in the wee hours of the morning and night seeking God, praying and crying out for your answer. Stop relying on the flesh to guide you. The flesh will cause you to make the wrong choice in picking your wife. Man of God, lean on the Holy Spirit and not lust. God may never just say it to you. He will however put a knowing down on the inside of you and keep pointing you in the right direction.

Now my brothers, let's talk! I am going to tell you how dangerous a woman can be if you mess over her or misuse her. You are probably saying, "Is she for real?"

Yes, I am, and some men know just what I am talking about. Man of God, when you turn a woman's world upside down, this displeases God. Stop making promises to women about marrying them. It is okay for you to change your mind but don't get upset when she starts tripping. You can change your mind but do it with decency.

Man of God, there are women out there who are generous and want to get married. These women have been told by older mothers and pastors that if they wait, God is going to send them a godly husband. These women have been praying, waiting and believing God for a husband. Man of God, don't show interest in a woman and start taking her to dinner, to the movies and to church and then say you two are only friends. In her mind and the mind of others, you are dating.

With all these things going on, you are preparing for marriage. She now has the mindset for marriage and you being her husband. After courting her like this, the woman could become very excited and anxious. She may start to share this information with her girlfriends. The wedding planning begins... then you, man of God, start to pull away. You stop calling as much, no more dates and dinners, and she is now going to church alone. After that rejection, you start to put her down and say that things between the two of you won't work out.

Man of God, when you do things like this, it shatters a woman's image of men who may really have an interest in a good woman. Then when a man who has real intentions comes along, she doesn't believe him. When a woman is hurt from a man rejecting her, it leaves a deep wound in her soul. Man of God, this is why it is important to wait, watch and pray before you proceed toward a woman's heart.

You can take a lesson from King David who got in trouble with Bathsheba. This interaction between David and Bathsheba caused him to do stupid things as well as take matters into his own hands. David sent for another man's wife who he had no intention of marrying. Even if she was not already married, the intentions were wrong. David wanted to kill the woman's husband and marry her when she became pregnant with his child. After David's plan failed, he tried to cover it up by trying to get her husband to sleep with her so he could think the baby was his. David did everything he could to conceal the sin he had committed. It is true, we all make mistakes but this sin you should avoid.

Fatal attraction can cost you the ministry God has given you. All of your dreams could suffer as well. Make sure your hookup is from God and not your flesh. Man of God, you have the choice to choose but choose to make godly decisions. Be like the men of old. Have a deep relationship with God. The things of this world were not back then. The way women dress, walk, talk and present themselves was much different than they are today. Holiness was a way of life for women back in the day. It appears as if women of today are moving away from holiness. Today's women don't care (not all of them). Some say, "I want him and I am going to get a him no matter what."

We cannot overlook the process of marriage and being found by your helpmate. Genesis reminds us that God told Adam that he was giving him a helpmate. Why would God say that it was not good for man to be alone? It is because God knew man needed someone to stand beside him and not rise above him.

God made the helpmate to be gentle and quiet to stand by man's side and allow him to lead. God created Adam to be referenced as "king." The role of the helpmate is to support her husband in decision making while trusting him to lead. This order that God ordained for marriage is strategic to avoid the fatal attraction syndrome.

Man of God, trust God. He will give you what you want and then some. If what you want is not based on lust but trusting God's Word, you will get what God created for you. It is very important that you get the woman God created for you to see your purpose fulfilled. When you choose the woman God has for you, she will know exactly how to care for you in all walks of your life. She will know how to accompany you in prayer, the bedroom and in every way.

The wrong woman can drain you and leave you feeling empty and feeling like less of a man. She will not build you up but tear you down; she cannot see in the spirit to help you make the right choices.

If you choose the wrong woman, you will begin to make her the center of attention and focus on her needs instead of God's needs. The need to focus on her ministry will be her priority while your ministry dies. She will say things like: "You don't care about my ministry," or "I had this ministry when I met you." The wrong woman will tell you what she thinks you want to hear to get what she wants and not what God has for her. She will step on whomever to get what she wants.

First John 5:14-15 is sometimes taken out of context. The Bible says that if we ask according to His will. Well once we become a new creature in Him, then we don't think or act the old way.

Let me say this: we are not supposed to anyway. If the carnal mind is still there, the spirit of jealousy can fall over the marriage. The wrong woman in your life may operate out of a place of jealousy. She may want to know your every move and whom you are talking to and about what. This type of woman can cause confusion in your life.

So many men today have forgotten to add God to the equation to the search of finding their wife. God wants to be a part of everything we do. He has already preordained our life and already knew what He has for us. He just wants us to pray to Him, for this helps us to develop a relationship with Him and it shows Him that we need and want Him to be in on every decision we make.

When times get hard, she will not support you but put you down. The right woman will stick by you through whatever happens. Believe it or not there are a lot of good men (men of God) going through this right now but are too prideful to admit they should have listened and prayed to God before they got married to a woman with the characteristics I've just described. My brothers, let down your pride and let God bring you healing through the process. Yes, you should have listened but you didn't; so forgive yourself because God has the right helpmate for you.

When you get this woman, if she is not God-ordained for your life, you will go through a storm and the fire before you get a season of rain and showers of blessings. I say to you, my brother, pray and seek God for that answer. God will sometimes put a knowing down on the inside of you. It is called the Holy Spirit; don't confuse it with lust. I believe that lust sometimes comes and overrides the Holy Spirit, which can lead to you making the wrong decision and marrying the one.

Her desire for you will become so strong that it can cause her to lust for you too. Her lust is a strong longing to be with you. She will not know exactly what she is feeling because it can be so overpowering and strong. Everything within her craves for you, including her body. Beware of the lustful woman and ask God for a praying woman. When you know she is the one, don't drag your feet knowing that she is fighting for her life trying to stay pure and holy. Paul said in 1 Corinthians 7:9 that it's better to marry than to burn.

God can still carry out every plan for your life; getting married will not stop Him. When you both know that you were created for one another, then proceed into marriage as God has ordained you to do.

First Corinthians 7:5 also says that when you are married, only abstain from sex for a season so Satan doesn't come and tempt you. This is for the married people: don't wait too long because that fire temptation will begin to burn like never before and you might not be able to put it out.

John 14:15

If ye love me, keep my commandments

Chapter 4

Sister Got Game

My brother, some sisters truly have game. I know that some of you guys know what I am talking about. A sister can either have good game or bad game. The game I am referring to is this: she knows how to seduce a brother. Through her actions, she knows what to say and what not to say. Man of God, you could be made to be a puppet on a string or just made a monkey from dealing with this type of woman. The actions of a sister playing games can include what she says, how she dresses and how she walks.

There is a pure walk, which would signifies holiness. This walk will tell you everything you need to know about her lifestyle and character.

The other walk, talk and the way she dresses will show signs of the Delilah spirit. The Delilah spirit will manipulate her way into your life. The Delilah walk will strip a man of his anointing. The same thing that happened to Samson will eventually happen to you. Delilah was used to find out all of Samson's secrets and especially where his strength dwelled. Once she found out, she took it all from him.

Brother, your anointing is your strength; Satan knows this and he wants to destroy it. He wants to destroy your anointing so that you do not fulfill the call of God over your life. His main goal is to take you out. Brother, I know you are thinking this cannot happen to you but it can; look at what happened to Samson. He asked God to give him strength to destroy the Philistines and God gave him his request but as a result, he died. My brother, don't die in your season of the Delilah spirit.

My brother, it is important that you seek God about her, take your time and pray awhile. There is nothing wrong with taking your time to find the woman God has ordained for your life. When you are in direct communion with God, you will find your helpmate and be married until death do you part. Allow God to select your wife and not your flesh.

When you do not wait, you will find yourself being baited by the enemy by way of a woman. The hook will be connected to a bait and she will begin to reel you in. If you allow God to bring that mate to you, you will then begin to see the beauty of God's will and how much better your life will be. When your true wife is presented to you, she will bring you so much joy. You will know she is truly from the Lord because she will serve you, love you, respect you and support you. She will be able to do these things because these things are already in her to give. God knows just what you need.

A woman who is not coming with games will adore you, not put you down. She will lift you up and always see the good in you. She understands that greater is HE that in you than he that is in the world. She knows what shall be and patiently waits for God to fulfil the Word concerning you. The woman who is not playing games will stay on her face for change to take place within both of you. The Word of God says that all things are possible to those who believe. Do you believe that all things are possible?

Man of God, God wants to give you a woman of God who will speak edifying words of support over your life. This sister will push you straight into your destiny. She will not try to rule you but will allow you to rule and reign in your rightful place as the head. Man of God, God wants to give you a woman who will celebrate you and not tolerate you. This sister will build you up and not tear you down. She will compliment you through words of encouragement no matter how bad it looks or seems. She will not call you names but will pray with you and for you.

One of the things I have found out about women in the last three to five years is that some women don't care if God has preordained a husband for them; they just want a man and any man will do. They do not care who they have to step on or step over or who they hurt, they just want a man. Many women proclaim to be holy but their actions are worldly. How some women treat other women shows no respect or fear of God. Many profess to be holy and godly women but when it comes to getting a man, it changes.

It is important to have the Holy Ghost. The Holy Ghost is a microscope, a magnifying glass, that gets down to the realness of a person. It will not allow you to hide. The Holy Spirit will reveal things that others try to hide. Nothing slips past the Holy Spirit. The Holy Spirit will expose who a person really is. My brother, check out the pureness of a woman's heart. The woman who likes to play games will try to convince you that she is the one for you. She just wants whatever she wants and desires that you fall prey to it.

She will not seek God to know for herself that you are the one. She will seek the word of others and go with that. A woman playing games doesn't care how she has to manipulate you; she just is after marriage. She wants you and is determined to make you hers. She is holding on to that worldly mentality.

In 1 John 5:14-15, it says that this is the confidence that we have in Him, that if we ask anything according God's will. According to this verse, we must understand that we have our petitions and must make them known unto God. A woman who doesn't understand this Bible verse will automatically think it means she can have any man she desires; but the truth is, she can have the man, God wills for her life.

Many women have grown tired and taken matters into their own hands. The tragedy of doing this and things not working out can cause one to want to throw in the towel. Many women move forward with getting a husband based on someone else's word. The flesh is leading instead of the Holy Spirit. Today in the church among the women of God, there is no more depth in them. The love and respect for one another is no more. It is all games and untruths towards one another.

The games they would play is laughing in one another's face then turning around and talking about each other.

I would like to tell you about some of the things that happened to me with sisters who played games within the church. First, let me say that if some of you sisters who did this are reading this book, you are already forgiven. God knew beforehand what was I what was going to happen so He let it take its course. For God knew the plans He had for me. The experience I went through allowed me to grow. If you are not guilty of any wrongdoings, then move on. I had doors shut in my face by the so called sister's. Lies were being told on me. I got calls in the middle of the night cursing me out. I would be in the pulpit ministering and they would turn the music up on me. I will stop there the rest coming in another book . These are a few things I encountered.

Proverbs 1:7

The fear of the Lord is the beginning of knowledge: but fools despise wisdom and instruction

Chapter 5

Man of God, Stop Tripping

I want to say this to the men of God who are pastoring, single and thinking about getting married: Your decision to get married must come from God's timing and not your own desire to be married. When we look at it from a biblical standpoint, show me where in the Bible it tell us that we must be married at a specific time in our life.

Getting married later in ministry will not mess up your purpose of pastoring. God said that he who findeth a wife findeth a good thing. Don't you think that God knows when to send her and when to present her to you? He is God and God alone.

He doesn't really need your help to do anything. It is just the way He uses us to present our soulmates requires to human souls. He needs to use people to bring about His promises upon the earth. Let's not think that His hands are short and He doesn't know what He has already ordained to take place in our life. Stop trying to do God's job for Him. We must allow Him to be God and show Himself mighty in all situations. Man of God, concerning marriage, what are you waiting for?

Just tell the truth: some of you are afraid to move forward and trust God this time and not yourself. Stop holding on to your past and move forward; stop making excuses. Stop saying it's the ministry and you are so into building the people that there is no room for God to bless you with a wife. You must be prepared for God to send you a wife to stand by your side and help execute the vision God has given you.

God said that it's not good that man be alone. He knew what you as men would face. He knew when he formed you in your mother's womb that you would be pastors, ministers and preachers. He knew the challenges you would face. He knew this would not be easy but hard, and even harder when faced with so much opposition from the world. God desires that you not fall but stand. For this very reason, he said that the woman is to be your helpmate and a good thing. She was created just for you and knows what you would need to be successful in the things of God.

The woman whom God has for you is to satisfy your every need. If you meet one who does not meet the criteria God has shown you, you must depart from her and flee. Tell her "bye" before you say, "I DO." If you fall outside of the will of God, your ministry will die from malnourishment. Your wife should bring life to your ministry and not death. Stay in the will of God when it comes to the things of God and marriage. What God has for you is for you. If you trust God like you say you do and have faith in God for your destiny, then you will not care so much about what man says about you getting married. Instead you will solely rely on God and the promises He has spoken over your life.

As a pastor, you belong to God and the people in your church belong to God. He has just given you charge to watch over them, shepherd them and oversee them while they are on this Christian journey. God adds to the church daily as he sees fit. Stop trying to control your destiny when God already ordained it. Seek God to know if it is time to date or be married. God said He would give you your heart's desires.

If it is your desire to be married or to date, then God will set it up because you only desire what God has already set into motion. Stop being afraid to let go and let God direct your path. You must give your entire life over to Him and let Him take full control.

You say you have passed from life unto death in Christ Jesus. It's no more you that liveth but Christ, that hope of glory, that lives within you. He doesn't want to be a part-time Father to you so you must be a full-time servant for Him. Make a decision today to let Him direct every step instead of the people that you lead. Believe it or not, the people you lead will never hand over complete control of their life to you.

My brother, I know that you are very important to God and He has so many blessings predestined for you. God does have a plan for your life. All you have to do is just find out what the plan is through prayer and His Holy Word. Man of God, become strong in God's Word and develop a prayer life. God say's He delighteth Himself in your prayers. This means it brings Him joy when we put our trust in Him to bring us through even when we do not understand His ways.

Man of God, stop tripping over what others say concerning you. God is strategic in everything He does. God created the heavens and the earth and fashioned them to operate in their own space and time. God said that the earth was void and without form. God's spirit moved over it and His voice caused it to move. It was He who spoke and everything was exactly as He commanded it to be. My brother, just know God uses you and works through you. We were purchased through His Son Jesus Christ's blood. It was and is Jesus who made the ultimate sacrifice, not us.

Surrender to His plan and will for your life and ministry. Let God work His work through you. Be a yielding man of God and not an unyielding one. Work what God has placed in you. If you enter into a relationship that you must keep hidden from others, then ask yourself: "What would Jesus do?" Do you both really have to hide from others what you feel for one another? If so, then ask yourself why this is. You do not need others' permission to love the person God has placed in your life. People will always have an opinion until Jesus comes back. Live for Christ; stop living for people and what they may say or do. Man of God, just believe God and obey Him. Once you obey Him, you will always win for you are a winner. You were created to win and have victory over the adversary.

Do you not think that the people of old didn't have anything to say when David, Jacob, Isaiah, Boaz and many other men got ready to marry? Don't think that everyone was in agreement with their choices or timing. Remember when Moses' brother Aaron and his sister Miriam complained about whom Moses had married? When they complained, God stepped in and caused them to become sick. God had already ordained the marriage. He designed it where they met in Midian and her father would give her to be Moses wife.

Zipporah had six other sisters (Exodus 2:16-21) that Moses could have picked from; however, God knew which one was right for him. God gave him eyes for Zipporah only. Moses could have said "no" but he didn't. I know some of you may try to get deep on me. I know that back in those days, the oldest daughter got married first. It does not state that she was the oldest. It said that the priest of Midian had seven daughters.

I know you're probably wondering why this chapter was titled Stop Tripping. The reason is to get your attention, my brother. It is to get you to move forward in what God said for you to do. It is an alarm for you to become more aware of what is ahead for you. My brother, let go and let God have his way in your life. Jesus' Spirit lives within you and it will not lead you wrong. You must have the Holy Spirit to lead you all to truth. Pray, believe and trust God for every move in your life.

Some will say God had it on delay. I say you have it on delay. The delay is your disobedience versus God's plan. If God ordained you to do something a specific way, He has already made provision for it to manifest. Stop forfeiting your destiny. God has not given you the spirit of fear but a sound mind to go and slay the giant that lies before you. Stand up and trust God. Trust Him for everything. You trust Him for others, now trust Him for yourself.

I know you may have been hurt before just like the sisters have; however, you must not let your past keep you from your future. As a man, you must learn to forgive, forget and move towards the mark of the high calling. Yes, you may have made a bad choice before but just remember the good and move on with God as your shield and buckler. As your sister, I can tell you that it is getting brighter. I see it. Give love another chance. Learn to trust, brother. Let God heal your wounds from the past. The delay is in you; move it out of your way and tell it to move in Jesus' name. God has many blessings planned for your life. Stop tripping and allowing the enemy in your life to hold you up.

Sometimes the enemy can be yourself. Stop holding yourself up and move. Stop making excuses for why you cannot go forward. Lay down your weapon for the battle is not yours; it belongs to the Lord. No matter how you try to do it on your own, know that He that has begun a new thing in your life will complete it. Go look in a mirror and declare yourself a Winner. Say it loud and with conviction that you will overcome everything that stands in your way. You are a Winner because God has predestined you to win.

Chapter 6

Just Keeping It Real

Now in this chapter, we will go deeper. I would like to just throw the hook out a little further and if this touches you in anyway, just say "oh my." I want to talk to the brothers who are just a little confused and don't seem to know what to do when you see a nice-looking woman and you know you have an eye for her. This is especially to the man in leadership whether you are a pastor, preacher, teacher or doorkeeper. If you meet a woman in or out your church and this woman catches your physical eye because of her beauty, just know this doesn't mean that God didn't open your eyes to see her.

If you are a man of God and you know you are, you should be aware if you are reacting out of the flesh or the spirit. Physical attraction will not last in a marriage but spiritual attraction will. I know when we are led with our flesh, we make a mess. When the spirit guides, we can then concede with the plans God has for man and his wife. When it is God that draws two people together, it is likely to endure the hard times of marriage. When God lives on the inside of two people, it makes a difference. When we are His, He takes away our desires and replaces it with His own desires.

Brother, know there is nothing wrong with being attracted to a sister; just don't allow lust to lead you astray from the Gospel of Jesus Christ. When a woman is well put together, it is hard not to see it. Truth be told, what you see in a woman, another man may not see it the way you do. For God gave it to you just that way to draw you to her. Brothers, you have to be delivered from your past relationships with other women before pursuing any woman who may become a prospect to be your future wife. Ask God to remove the hang-ups you may have. You cannot go into another relationship thinking all women are the same. One or two bad apples don't spoil the whole basket.

Unresolved hurt can have you going through cycles of ups and downs. These cycles of past relationships can make you feel unstable in your mind. The unstableness will cause you to look over what God has right before your face. Brother, you know what you like and God knows it too, and that is why He put that sister together the way He did; He wants to give you your heart's desires. God wants you to be a sure that what He has placed before you is what you will be content with until death do you part. This way you are no longer having eyes for any other women.

Have you ever seen a man with a woman and you said to yourself, "What does she want with him? He is so ugly"? Have you ever seen a man with a woman and said, "He must be blind. I don't know what he sees in her"? What God sees and what we see is two different things. Since we are looking through Jesus' eyes, all we are supposed to see is the heart of Jesus.

God knows what you need, my brother. He puts it together nicely for you to enjoy the benefits of marriage. Stop fighting God for your life. He knows you better than you know yourself. Man of God, stop prolonging what is yours by doubting and drifting back into your past; please do not miss your blessings. Don't miss out on your good, good, good thing. Don't miss out on the very thing God knows you want: a godly woman. Stay in constant prayer and ask God to reveal to you the path He has for you. I promise that sticking close to God will pay off.

God wants you to have the best. All of God's daughters are the best. There is one who was created just for you. Even if you are divorced or your wife has passed away, God can still design another. God is checking to see if your heart is connected to Him or to your own fleshy ways and desires.

Proverbs 3:5

Trust in the LORD with all your heart and lean not on your own understanding.

Chapter 7

The Heart

Well it's about that time again, Man of God. It is time for you to allow God to do a thorough check-up on your heart. It is time for Him to see if your heart is connected to His or if your heart is lusting after the fleshy things you desire. God wants to regulate your heart so that it functions from a place of purity.

I know it to be true. As I was writing this book, I was standing in faith on a promise that God had given me. Sometimes in the face of promise, I wanted to give up and say, "Lord, I cannot do this and my heart is not going to be able to endure this test of faith." While spending countless nights crying over the promise, I was reminded that God can help me do all things through Him. God strengthened my heart and told me I was going to make it through this process and accomplish the promise He had placed in me. God knew the enemy would try to weaken me so that my purpose would not be fulfilled.

The promise God gave me was my true strength. The promise is what kept me going. When you want something bad enough, you will stretch yourself beyond your human capability. It takes perseverance to wait for the promises of God to manifest. The trying of your heart really strengthens your faith in God. As I spent mornings and nights, crying out to God to being His promise for this book to come to pass, the pressure was intense. Through this process, God regulated my heart that His promise over my life would not be miscarried.

My brother, while checking your heart, make sure that it does not have any clogs or anything that stops it from beating to Jesus' rhythm. Make sure that the heart you have is ever-changing and you do not have the same heart you had five years ago. If your heart needs fixing, call the heart surgeon; His name is Jesus. Make sure you have a heart to treat your sisters in the Lord right.

Sometimes you have to look back over your life and review your experiences with women. Whether you encountered women in church or the nightclub, you need to have a heart to treat women with respect and dignity. Yes, I said the nightclub because some of you are still not fully delivered and are clubbing in secret. This has to stop because satisfying your flesh is wrong. Stop feeding that lust monster that lives on the inside of you. God wants to expose what is really in your heart and that tainted anointing you are carrying.

God will not allow you to walk over His precious daughters. Please do not misuse them and their feelings for you. Remember He has placed a heart in His daughters to love and He will guard it at all cost.

I am now going to ask that some of you brothers do this heart check and see if the "dog mentality" is still in you. The dog mentality that may have attached itself to you is full of pride, disrespect and a need to control women whom you may feel are subservient to you. My brother, stop having women chase you; they should be chasing after the heart of God. Cancel that dog mentality that lives on the inside of you. You must surrender everything that is not clean and righteous over to God. Place your heart over to God at the altar and get delivered from your infirmities.

Like a car engine. When you first purchase the car brand new, the engine is good and working with

NO problems. As years go by, that engine has to be overhauled. When the engine has to be replaced, it has to be tested to ensure it is going to work properly and you will not have any problems going forward. God knows how to regulate your heart as well. He can take your heart that is not working properly and replace it with one that does.

My brother, I want you to stop right here and take 10 minutes to think about the things you may have done to your sisters. Some of you it may take more than 10 minutes. However long it takes, my brother, just repent and let God heal your heart. Brother, knowing that you had no interest in a woman to marry her is inconsiderate of her time and feelings. How would you feel if this was done to you? Brother, how would you feel if you started to develop feelings for a woman and she dropped you without notice with no reason why?

My brother, remember that whatever you sow, you shall reap. If you were just being nice to a sister and she took it the wrong way, I am not talking to you. I am talking to the brothers who knew a sister was head over heels in love with you and you chose to play with her feelings anyway. Be careful with a sister when you tell her you only want to be friends. A woman may have been hurt and saw something in you that gave her a sense of security. The heart of a woman is fragile. It is a place where you can love and be loved or a place to hurt others or be hurt. Love can bring peace into someone's life or chaos. It is important that you do a heart check daily. It is key to allow God to examine it every day.

There is another issue of the heart that I would like to talk about: Past hurt should not hold you back from loving again. Some brothers say they do not want to be married again and they are now comfortable in singleness. God desires for men to have wives. You must search deep within yourself and you will find that there is still some residue of your past hindering you from moving forward.

The spirit of fear is also another reason why you procrastinate about marriage. Brother, you say you trust God for everything but when it comes to this particular matter, you stop trusting God. The problem is you want to do it your way and then apply God's name to it. My brothers, it does not work that way. The heart is a place of intimacy. It is also a place of secret sins. You must learn to let God have total control. The secret place is a place where you hide your hurt, pain and disappointments. The heart is the area that God wants to invade but He wants you to allow Him to do so.

Jesus cares for you. He will take good care of your heart and make sure it is in the right hands. I guess some of you say, "How does she know what is going on with a man when she is a woman?" As a woman, I have been through some things—not knowing that all the time, God was setting me up to write this book. The Father wants you to forget about your past and press forward forth into that which He has called you to in every area of your life. My brother, when you are a yielded vessel to God and not your own ways and thoughts, He will begin to put things in order for your life. Search out your ways and thoughts to see if they are of God.

The blood that filters out of the heart is the same blood that runs through it. What I am saying is that God wants to purify it and allow the blood of Jesus Christ to flow through your heart. Man of God, there is no hidden or secret places that God cannot touch, fill or heal when hurt. I know all about you being told by your father (if you had one in the home) to not cry because men don't cry. My brother, you can still be strong even if you open up and allow God's healing power to heal, fill and touch you in every area of your life, especially your heart. The truth is real men do cry.

Be strong and let God heal you and fill you up where you are empty and touch that wound that needs to be healed. Jesus gave His life so you could be free from the baggage and bondage of your past. If covered up, the baggage of life can continue to leave you in a place of hurt and pain. God is saying to remove the bandage and let the blood flow (pain and hurt). The Lord can heal you from the inside out.

While being taught to be strong, you sometimes miss what real love is and how it is supposed to feel. After surrendering your old heart to God, you will have a heart of God. Don't allow this change to make you afraid and pull back. Fear could be a sign that something is wrong with your heart. Fear will cause you to not let go of your past. Stop trying to fake it until you make it. I am going to pause right here for a minute to say something to the pastors out there: Pastors, you are the main ones who will cover up your hurts and disappointments. Man of God, you need healing like everyone else. God called you to lead, but He never said that you would not bleed a little along the way.

Pastor, your members need a whole, healed leader to care for them, pray for them and care for their spirit. When you are not healed and whole, it will affect your relationship within the Body of Christ and within your marriage. There is a saying that says hurt people, hurt people; and without allowing God to heal you, you could possibly hurt others. Be careful whom you allow to minister to your healing. The right covering is important. The heart is in need of a checkup; let the presence of God consume your life.

Watch and see the big difference that love can bring to your life. Everyone around you will see the difference. There is a place in God that He desires all of us to reach, and this is a place of abundant peace. When love is in your life, it changes the atmosphere. My brother, let God clean and purify your heart, and pain by healing your inner disappointments. What God really wants to do is give you a new heart and get rid of the one that is infected and all messed up.

Allow Him right now to enter into your heart and transform your life. Close your eyes right now and begin to ask God to give you a new heart. Become transparent with God and tell Him what you want and need. Let him know how much you want to be healed and made new. Stay right there in the presence of God until you get what you need. Block out everything around you. Turn off the phone, TV and computer. Remove all the distractions and wait for God.

James 1:17

Every good and perfect gift is from above, coming down from the Father of the heavenly lights, who does not change like shifting shadows.

Chapter 8

Change is Coming

Change will come to you, man of God, if you allow God's Word to change you from the inside out. God wants to change his "sons of thunder." Let God change you through this book. My prayer is that you will be better equipped in waiting on God to send your ordained wife. I know we all want to be married and have that lifelong partner. In order to have that successful marriage, you must be aligned with God's plan.

Brother, I know that waiting for that special someone can be hard. I know you may say that God has not showed you anyone but in reality, He has. Sometimes the person who is right in front of you is overlooked due to your hang-ups and other issues that may be surrounding you at the time. My brother, it is all about God's timing and not your timing. When you operate outside of God's timing, you will find that things you ask God for can be held up and delayed. God loves you. You are His son and He desires that you have the woman that He has kept especially just for you.

I know sometimes you may be hooked up with the wrong one and things don't work out, but don't give up on God because of your own mistakes. God still loves you and He desires that you get married. Put your past behind you, let go of the past and focus on what lies ahead of you. I understand that no one wants to be hurt or disappointed but on this journey called life, we all will experience disappointment along the way.

My brother, it is up to you to let go of everything that hinders you from progressing in the things of God. When seeking the things of God, you must get up and position yourself to hear from Him so that you can receive the blessings He has for you. Stop making excuses, stop saying God doesn't want you to get married when the Word says that it is not good for man to be alone.

God does not tempt His people. He said that when you are tempted, it is of your own lust (1 Corinthians 10:13). Paul said that he wished that all were like him; but if you can't contain yourself then it is better to be married than to burn (1 Corinthians 7:9). This scripture simply says that when you have the desire to have sex, it should be fulfilled by your wife. Sex outside of marriage is sinful. Yes, I said it. Sex is something many do not want to discuss in the Body of Christ.

Brother, it is better to marry than to burn in your desires. Taking cold showers will not always put out that fire that seems to be burning within you. Many of you have lustful thoughts that cause your fire to burn even hotter, looking at women and having ungodly visions of them with their clothes off or even envisioning yourself having sex with them. If a woman is not good enough to marry, then please do not lie with her. Remember brother, you will be held accountable even for your thoughts. Consider the heart of a woman instead of her body.

Brother, stop thinking about yourself and think about the woman and what she may be going through. I don't care how steamy and hot you are for this woman; if you do not have a heart to love her and make her your wife, then I suggest you be honest with her and leave her alone. Don't go after a woman to just get into her pants. If your heart is right and you know she is ordained to be your wife, then do the right thing and consult God then marry her. If you are unsure then do not proceed.

Pray and find out to ensure you will be doing the right thing and not a fleshy thing. If you have mislead her along the way, ask for forgiveness and acknowledge that you messed up.

Brother, don't be afraid to cancel a wedding if you know that God has not given you full consent to move forward in marriage. It will hurt her, I know, but she will thank you later when she sees it was for the better on both sides. For God knows what is best for you. Man of God, don't be prideful; admit you made a mistake. Moving ahead of God can come with a costly price. If you move forward without God's consent, it may be good for two or three months or even years; however, the real "self" will come out and it may not be what you expected.

When seeking, looking and hoping for a wife, do it with much prayer and fasting. Your lifetime partner can either make you or break you. Do it

God's way and not your way or by the world's standards. For God says in all your ways acknowledge him and he shall direct your path. God does not want to be left out of His sons' very important life decisions. It is like your real father and mother in the natural. It would be right to go to them and tell them of your decision to get married, get their blessings and invite them to the wedding. It is God who formed you in your mother's womb and foreknew you and all the plans your life would entail. It was Him who had already planned your life out and He desires that they all come to pass.

Get into the presence of God. Spend time and allow Him to move for you. Allow Him to speak to you and trust Him to answer. For there is so much in you that God wants to birth out if you will let Him. Where you are right now may not look good to you but God already knows what He called you to. God is knocking at the door of your heart. He is trying to open the door of your past. Allow God to heal you from the inside out. Ask him to heal your hurt, rejection, pain and disappointments.

I know men are told from a boy that men don't cry. If you're created in God's image, just know that Jesus wept. God feels what we feel. If we hurt, He hurts. There is nothing wrong with crying. Some of you think life is over because you have gotten hurt by past relationships. I say to you, let go and let God fill that spot of pain, hurt, rejection and disappointment up with His healing power. For only God can truly heal you.

Count this experience as one of life lessons that you learn from and don't hold it inside to haunt you. Release her and let it go. Don't get stuck in thinking that every woman is the same; we are not all alike. Through every experience you go through concerning relationships and marriage,

God will bring you out and show Himself mighty. Whatever seems hard and dead, God can give life to it. God is trying to develop his character in you. It will sometimes allow humility to grow within you too.

There is something about a man of God that is so different from a worldly man. A man of God should show signs of strength, power and authority. He should know how to lead, love as well as listen and obey the voice of God. These characteristics are true signs of a man of God. God wants you to operate in His image so that when you do get married, you will be in position to lead and not have your wife leading you. The woman should walk alongside you and not behind you. God has placed you, man of God, as the one to lead according to His Word.

When you are in the right position to lead, you will not be connected with the wrong spirit (woman) that will delay your purpose and make you feel less than a man. Man of God, you need a woman who will allow you to lead, and push and encourage you to lead even through difficult situations. The woman God has for you will truly build you up in every way. She will know how to keep you happy so you have no desire to look or go anywhere else.

There was a pastor from New Orleans and his wife preached a message titled "Do Your Thing and Do it Right to the Women." She let us know through her teachings that we must care for our husbands and treat them right. She wanted us to understand that if we didn't take care of our husband, somebody else would for us. This message made a great impact on my life even though I am not married. It helped prepare me for my husband-to-be and how to care and love him. This particular message has equipped me with some tools on how to minister to my husband when God allows that man to come forth.

The man was not made for the woman but the woman for the man. For God created Adam first and then saw that Adam was lonely. This is why having a prayer life is very important. Through your prayer life, you allow God to change you. It is important that you get the right spouse. Make sure you get a woman of God and not just a sex toy, for it will surely not last.

The change that God is going to bring into your life is going to cause your tree to be full and overflowing. The overflow that will overtake you will require you to get baskets to receive it all. The change coming your way, Man of God, will produce blessings from the north, south, east and west. People around you will surely know that God is with you. When you open your mouth and speak, it will produce God's blessings unto you from the Heaven unto Earth.

God wants to cause you to be explosive in the Kingdom. He wants to blow you up so that you will have a powerful testimony afterwards. This change will help to draw others to Christ. This change will bring forth the love of God so others may see it and want to have a relationship with Him.

Matthew 7:7 says knock and it shall be opened unto you. If you knock, it will be opened unto you. For God wants to do it for you. It is time you knock into your ordained place through prayer. God is waiting for you to take a close look at where you are and where you would like to be. God wants to give you a complete makeover for His glory. This place of change will bring a great love for God and the things of God. It will help you learn the difference between His voice and your own voice.

Even the greatest men of God in the Bible went through the process of change. Jacob wrestled with God but he came out changed for the better.

New beginnings means there is an opportunity of letting go of your past or even what happened last week. Whatever it is, you must allow God to heal your old wounds. Stop covering them up and not allowing them to heal. You must deal with your past experiences and not allow them to mess up your blessings. Let go my brother and let God complete you. When you walk in obedience to God, good things will manifest.

Your prayer life is the foundation. The opening up of your mouth will be like a trumpet blowing unto Zion. Everybody will know that you have been with God in the holiest of holies. Obeying God brings great blessings upon you. Before you were saved, you were use to running things, picking and doing whatever you wanted to do. The anointing over your life signifies that you have been bought with the blood of Jesus. You no longer belong to yourself but are indebted to Christ Jesus. It is time to pull away from the world's systems and doing things the way the world does it. It is much easier for you to yield to the will of God and not fight the process that He has ordained over your life.

The process can take a awhile or it can be over in a night. It depends on how badly you want it. Are you willing to stay up all night before the Lord and cry out until He changes your situation as He did Jacob? What about the way He did David when he sinned against God? David laid out before the Lord until God moved and forgave him. By laying out on your face before the Lord, you must come before the Lord with a repenting heart.

The Lord said that He will not despise a broken and contrite heart (Psalm 51:17). This is the first step to being changed for His glory. Change has happened in the heart of other men of God so I know it is possible for you. The key to change taking place is submission to the process of deliverance. After deliverance takes place, you can then become a life-changer in the Kingdom of God. This is what Jesus was talking about in Matthew 5:13-16 when He said that we are the salt of the earth but if the salt loses it saltiness, how can it be made salty again? The essence of salt is that you are the flavor that is needed in the earth.

The second thing is that you must know who you are in God. Knowing who you are in God helps to produce change as well. When you know who you are in God, you will spend more time in meditation thinking on who God said you were and where you are headed in life. The enemy always has a plan against you but it is up to you, man of God, to counter act his plan and focus on the plan of God for your life. You must stop trying to do things your way. Get in the presence of the Lord and let Him make the changes in you. All you have to do is confess and release while God does the rest.

God loves and cares so much for you right where you are right now. Our relationship with God is as if you are with your children and you want to know where they are and what they are doing. God feels the same way you do about your own children. He loves you and wants to protect you at all cost. This accountability to God increases your relationship with your future wife and others. When you are accountable to God first, you can then be accountable to others.

Accountability to God is focusing on Him through prayer and studying his Holy Word. Do not neglect God. You have to make time for Him in season and out of season. Submit to Him and allow Him to make the change in you. You may be saying, "I don't need to change and I am fine the way I am." The truth be told, you need God to make a lot of changes in you. God will in no way violate His own laws concerning your free will. My brother, right where you are, lay aside your pride and stubbornness. Seek God the way the Lord almighty wants you to.

One of the biggest problems with some men is that they do not listen to women. We have a voice that needs to be heard. Sometimes how we say things can make situations more difficult, but then there are some men who don't want to listen to a woman and don't respect her opinion. Remember God has placed a word in the woman's belly too.

It is all in how she handles herself in delivering the message to a man. Some men must allow a woman to give birth to a word that may help him in life. Man of God, do not try to stop her but instead, help her. When a woman has a word, she has to release it when it is all locked up inside of her.

Man of God, when it is time, it's just time. When a baby is ready to be born, you cannot stop that baby from coming into the world. You cannot tell a baby to wait when it is in transition. God's timing is key. God's timing has its appointed time. There is no delay in God. Delay is within you. Delay is brought on by disobedience in wanting to keep things flowing our way. We have to stop tagging God in things He has nothing to do with. We have to stop putting God's name in things He hasn't or will not endorse. We've got to get over our own plans and putting God's name on it. We must stay close to God's heart when seeking the heart of God's daughter. Brothers, it is time to Stop Playing with a Sister's Heart.

Conclusion

I wrote this book in 2003. God knew that this was going to be needed to help myself and other women who had placed our hearts in the hands of the wrong men. I had hosted several women conferences and had heard from so many women about how they had been hurt by the men in the church. This book was designed to bring deliverance to the men and healing to the women of God who may have been hurt.

The man who hurt my heart and other women was a pastor. He was playing malicious games with all of our hearts. He would tell me one thing and tell the others something else. I am not going to go deep cause I want to save some for my next book. I want to shed light on the seriousness and dangerousness of playing with a sister's heart.

I met this man before going to Chicago. I went to visit his church with a friend. While at this service, the power of God hit me like a ton of bricks and I began to dance prophetically under the anointing of God. While dancing, I was told by my friend that he was watching me. While visiting with another sister, he gave me his number and we became friends (or so I thought). At the time, I was unaware that he was on the hunt—for a woman, that is.

From time to time, I would call him because I was going through stuff with the women in the church in Chicago. My spiritual mother advised me to stop calling him because he wanted me for himself. I obeyed her and stopped calling him. When I returned to Florida, I moved back to my home in Leesburg.

After moving back to Jacksonville, I went to this pastor's office and talked with him. He then informed me that he was engaged to be married. I gave him my blessings and said, "I will pray for the marriage to work out."

It wasn't until 2013 that everything came to a head. There were several women who got hurt as a result of his choices. He made a public announcement on social media that he had found his queen, and she was the woman God had chosen for him. One of the women he was involved with actually took her own life after reading his post on Facebook. She was so hurt that she hung herself and left a note.

He had played with my heart as we were seeing one another and he was still seeing the woman he was engaged to marry but had called it off.

Then he married the other woman he was involved with whom he had told me he didn't want. He was playing with the heart of at least three women. There may have been others but I am not sure.

I too was hurt over his behavior but I thank God that He kept me and I did not succumb to the suicide demon. He did not take responsibility for the other woman's suicide. He stated it was not his fault that she took her life. I later found out that he was still seeing her and taking money from her as well. It is sad that a sister had to take her life and leave her three children behind all because a man played with her heart and she thought her life would be over. She thought life was not worth living if she could not have him. He played with her heart and threw it away like a rag doll. She could not bear it.

The weight of the hurt, shame and disappointment was her affliction and it took her life. I can imagine she felt like a fool because she had been played by a man of God. She probably never expected a man of God to treat her like this.

I personally could not bear still being in the same city as he and his new wife. I prayed and God allowed me the opportunity to move to Atlanta to receive my healing, and God also allowed the pain to go away. We were the prey to this pastor on the hunt. He pounced on us as if we were nothing. I was confused and all messed up for a while, but God kept me through it all. He brought me to a safe and sound place in my mind. There could have been more lives lost because of this man of God's actions.

This encounter in my life is why I had to write this book. I had to tell this story so the next woman wouldn't have to go through what me and others had to experience.

God had a plan for my life and He saw fit that His plan was going to be fulfilled. Writing this book is part of the purpose God has for me.

Author Bio

Shane'tta Rodmon is the Apostle and Overseer of Yeshua Shekinah Global Ministries, Inc. She is the mother of two sons, Jason Scott and Wille Sapp, Jr., and two grandsons, Matthew and Isaiah Sapp. Apostle Shane'tta Rodmon was raised in Leesburg, Florida, by the late Mother Ida Mae Rodmon and her father Isaiah Rodmon, Stepmother – Betty Rodmon.

Apostle Rodmon lives her life to glorify God and uplift the Kingdom by preaching, teaching, praying, hosting conferences, doing outreach and so much more. Apostle Rodmon hopes that her ministry of writing will help men and women to be healed and delivered from the hurt and pain that may dwell inside their heart.

Author Contact Information

Email: ShanettaRodmon@att.net

Facebook: Shanetta Rodmon

Yeshua Shekinah Global Ministries , Inc.

Becoming Women of Power

Made in the USA
Columbia, SC
16 April 2019